This Book Belongs To:

....

Acknowledgements

Thank you to all of the people who have helped me, many of whom will remain unnamed. Special thanks to Mary Kole, Patricia Ross, Pastor Alero Igiehon, Mrs Funmi Ayodele, and my family. I am grateful for your support in bringing this book to life. All the honour and praises to God for His inspiring Word.

Kids' Mini Psalm Book Series Vol. 3
Blessed and Beautiful Tree: Psalm 1 *(with Psalm 121)*

Text Copyright © 2024 Tayo Oshaye
Illustrations © 2024 Yana Popova

First Edition
ISBN: 978-1-9993736-4-1 (softcover)
ISBN: 978-1-9993736-5-8 (hardcover)
ISBN: 978-1-9993736-3-4 (e-book)

Published by:

Tayo Oshaye Publishing
Aberdeen, Scotland, United Kingdom
www.joyfulpsalmskids.com

Printed in the UK

This book uses fictional characters to reflect on the themes from the biblical Psalms. Readers are encouraged to use this and similar resources for literature purposes only. The Holy Bible remains the most reliable source of guidance in God's Word. Unless otherwise indicated, scriptures quoted from the Holy Bible, New International Reader's Version, copyright © 1986, 1988, 1999, 2015 by Tommy Nelson. Used by permission. (https://www.bible.com/bible/110/PSA.1.NIRV)

Hymns and songs are from the public domain.
Tayo Oshaye is the writer of the "Trees Friendship Chorus".

Kids' Mini Psalm Book Series Vol. 3

Blessed and Beautiful

Psalm 1 (with Psalm 121)

Written by
Tayo Oshaye

Illustrated by
Yana Popova

Prologue

"Fill us with your love every morning. Then we will sing and rejoice all our lives." (Psalm 90:14, ICB)

Song[1]

1. I've got peace like a river,
I've got peace like a river,
I've got peace like a river in my soul.
I've got peace like a river,
I've got peace like a river,
I've got peace like a river in my soul.

2. I've got love like an ocean,
I've got love like an ocean,
I've got love like an ocean in my soul.
I've got love like an ocean,
I've got love like an ocean,
I've got love like an ocean in my soul.

3. I've got joy like a fountain,
I've got joy like a fountain,
I've got joy like a fountain in my soul.
I've got joy like a fountain,
I've got joy like a fountain,
I've got joy like a fountain in my soul.

[1]*A public domain hymn. Scripture references: Isaiah 48:7, Isaiah 61:3, Isaiah 66:12, Galatians 5:22.*

Prelude

Psalm 1 (A Psalm of David)[2]

1. Blessed is the person who obeys the law of the Lord. They don't follow the advice of evil people. They don't make a habit of doing what sinners do. They don't join those who make fun of the Lord and his law.

2. Instead, the law of the Lord gives them joy. They think about his law day and night.

3. That kind of person is like a tree that is planted near a stream of water. It always bears its fruit at the right time. Its leaves don't dry up. Everything godly people do turns out well.

4. Sinful people are not like that at all. They are like straw that the wind blows away.

5. When the Lord judges them, their life will come to an end. Sinners won't have any place among those who are godly.

6. The Lord watches over the lives of godly people. But the lives of sinful people will lead to their death.

[2]*Psalm 1:1–6 (https://www.bible.com/bible/110/PSA.1.NIRV), New International Reader's Version.*

A long time ago, God, the Creator, planted five trees—Firi Firtree, Pinely Pine, Larry Cedar, Oaklan Oak, and Juniper Broomley—among other trees in Edenwild Forest in a land far away. The great river, Deep Spring, flowed through Edenwild Forest, nurturing the trees and allowing each to grow deep roots and powerful branches. However, the occasional storm that swept through the forest posed a threat, causing harm to the trees.

Larry Cedar grew incredibly tall, surpassing all other trees in Edenwild. His roots were strong.

All the birds wanted to put their nests on Larry's boughs. Squirrels found joy in climbing his expansive branches. Even giraffes enjoyed resting under his comforting shade. Larry's shade was better than any other tree in the forest.

Larry flourished, standing as the most elegant tree in the entire forest. The other trees in Edenwild aspired to be like Larry Cedar, but none could match his beauty. He became the envy of the entire forest.

Pinely tried her best to grow as tall as Larry, but she couldn't.

Larry Cedar became famous.

He thought, *Birds compete to nest on my branches, giraffes seek shade under my canopy with their friends, and squirrels find my boughs the ideal spot. No tree in the forest comes close to what I offer!*

As the morning dawned, Deep Spring flowed through the forest, and the birds awoke with the stirring sunrise.

"Long live the land of Edenwild," proclaimed Deep Spring.

"Thank God for this beautiful warm day," said Oaklan. "Bless good ol' Deep Spring! Will you pass by my roots today?" asked Firi, the fir tree.

"I would love to, but I graciously follow the path that the Lord leads. I will flow towards the radiant cedar and channel my streams through the forest. If you are on my path today, it will be a blessing to see you," replied Deep Spring.

"Go on, flow, Deep Spring, and let God's will be done," said Firi.

Young Pinely disliked frequently having to wait for Deep Spring's flow. She was learning to get closer to the water's path.

"Do you not supply the needs of the trees, Deep Spring? You should happily tend to every living tree in this forest. Then we can all grow as tall and be as radiant as your special tree," said Pinely.

"Hang on in there, my pine tree," replied Deep Spring. "I will come to you today."

"Nature's talent show is just around the corner. That's my best event of the year!" said Juniper.

"The birds will be singing at the evening chorus of the trees at six o'clock," said Oaklan. "They are rehearsing for nature's talent show."

"It's going to be a good day! My favourite part of the show is the woodland contest. I can't wait to see everyone in their most gorgeous look," said Firi.

"I've pruned my branches ready for the day. I want to be the star of nature's woodland contest. I'm next to be named the most beautiful tree of Edenwild!" said Pinely.

"No trees can beat Larry Cedar to this. Everyone loves him!" said Firi.

That afternoon, all the trees of the forest dressed to look their best.

Oaklan said to Pinely, "Your needles look trimmed and regal."

"I am going for the win, my friend," said Pinely.
"It'll take much effort, friend," said Firi. "You can count on that!"

"I can't wait to show how strong I am!" said Oaklan.

Larry was being dressed by the landscape gardeners. He showed off his lovely branches and ornamental needle-like leaves.

"I'm still the most elegant," said Larry.

"You've got beauty and finesse!" replied Firi.

"I'll be keeping my winning streak endlessly!" said Larry.

"But I am almost as tall as Larry and have similar needles and cones," argued Pinely. "Why does he win every time, and I don't get picked?"

"Hey! I am Edenwild's pride, and you don't want to compete with me in this woodland. You can try, but . . ."
"I can look my best by fluffing up my needles and cones, and I will win!"

Pinely thought, *I want to be awarded the most stunning tree and win the supermodel medal this time. I want to shine and be the brightest in Edenwild. But it seems too difficult. Who can help me? Why was I planted here? Does God really care? I think he doesn't.*

As nature's woodland talent show drew closer, the trees grew very ex-cited, except for one.

Pinely expressed, "I don't like my cones. I want them to look like Larry Cedar's. All the animals like him."

Larry retorted, "Don't try to be like me. I am the beauty of the land. No one can take my place in this forest."

"That's not true. Why did you say something so unfair?" cried Pinely. "No one cares about your looks, Pinely!" said Larry. "If you can't cope with losing, I'll advise you not to come to this contest."

Firi calmly responded, "It doesn't bother me whether my cones get picked or not. I'm grateful to participate. I'm just going to enjoy my day."

Larry continued to boast all day   to the trees, leaving Pinely angry.

Pinely came up with a plan. "I need to extend my roots towards Deep Spring's channel so that I get her nurturing."

"I'll stretch my branches to stop you. I'll shake the ground with my trunk, and all your cones will fall off. You'll be the foolish tree!" Larry countered.

"Why did you say something so unfair?" said Pinely.

This led to an argument between the two trees.

"Stop it! That is not a clever idea," Juniper intervened. "You guys will get into trouble if you are not kind to each other."

"Okay, I'm not coming to the talent show," Pinely said. "I'm leaving Edenwild today!"

Larry grinned, saying, "Leave!"

"I wish I could be taken to another forest, somewhere far away!" Pinely grumbled.

"Stop it, please!" said Juniper, leaning into the fray. "Pinely, you look radiant and fabulous."

"It doesn't matter whether I win or not. I am special and proud of myself in many ways," said Oaklan.

"It's just nature's talent show anyway! Your job is to serve the birds and animals," said Firi.

"But I don't feel as impressive as Larry," sulked Pinely.

"Sometimes life feels that way," said Juniper.

"Choose your battles wisely, Pinely. Do you know that God loves you no matter what?" said Oaklan.

"Everyone is beautiful in their own way. Let God's will be done," said Firi.

Pinely wiped her tears and smiled at them.

"That's really true. We are all special. I am a pine tree, and I will be presenting myself as the lovely pine tree that I am."

"I am the only beautiful, exceptional, and extraordinary tree. Who do you think you are?" asked Larry.

"I am a good tree and a masterpiece of the Lord of all creations," replied Pinely. "I am precious and beautiful to God who made me."

"You are the worst, Pinely, and don't let anyone fool you," said Larry.

"Be quiet, Larry," said Oaklan. "There's hope for everyone at the show." Oaklan shared the beloved Bible story of creation, recounting when God Almighty made the universe and everything in it. He reminded the trees that God saw everything He made as good.

"As it was in the beginning, every one of us—Pinely, Juniper, Firi, Larry Cedar, and even myself—is an amazing wonder of creation!"

Larry Cedar wasn't convinced at first, but gradually, he agreed.

"I am sorry for being mad at you, Pinely," said Larry. "I just didn't want you to be as good as me. You really are a shining star, and I will be as happy if you win the contest."

"I will be as happy if you win too, Larry," said Pinely.

"Something wonderful is happening here, and I hope we all accept this as change for good," said Oaklan.
They began to sing cheerfully, "Friends forever, blessed forever, that's who we are!"[3]

[3]"The Trees Friendship Chorus", written by Tayo Oshaye (2023).

The day of nature's talent show finally arrived, and at sunrise, the birds began to sing.
Firi, Pinely, Oaklan, and Juniper were all present, eager for nature's woodland contest.

Larry spoke boldly and charmingly, "I am Cedar, the tall tree. Everyone would like to be like me. In this place, I make a big difference. All creatures great and small marvel at my beauty. I am the place they go for shelter. I am the place from which they see the horizon. I am the place they seek for peace and quiet. I am the place to be in this forest.[4] There's no other tree or shrub in all of Edenwild that possesses the same power, elegance, and greatness as me."

[4]Psalm 60:10

Next, Firi stepped forward. "I am the beloved fir tree, made of noble wood.[5] I've got candlestick cones that make the most wonderful home decorations."

Next, it was Juniper's turn. "I have very tough roots that can endure any condition, even in the desert.[6] The fuel derived from me burns cleanly. My unique berries are used to produce aromatic oil and spicy sauces."

Oaklan went next. "I am an oak. I provide very durable wood that resists insect and fungal attacks. Some friends even call me 'Oak of righteousness' because people who honour God are strong like an oak. [7] I am planted here to display God's glory."

Finally, it was Pinely's turn.

"I am the green pine tree, a fruitful tree.[8] I've got lovely pine nuts to make delicious syrups, and my cones and branches brighten children's days."
The other trees came forward and did their best as well.

[5] Isaiah 55:13. / [6] 1 Kings 19:4. / [7] Isaiah 61:3 / [8] Isaiah 60:13.

The bird choir sang and danced throughout the woods. The monkeys, chimpanzees, and sloths gave their performances. The other animals paraded, two by two.

At the end, the judges gathered and announced the results.

"The award for the most stunning tree goes to a supermodel. His fragrance is the most pleasant. He gives the most powerful perfume that repels bugs and moths. He is the best softwood around! His towering height attracts every bird to his branches. He is a beauty to behold, the place to go for shelter, the place from which to see the horizon, the place to find peace and quiet, the place to be in this forest. We haven't found any other tree or shrub in all of Edenwild that is as powerful, elegant and great as . . . Larry Cedar."

All the trees clapped for Larry!

The judges also presented other awards. Oaklan received recognition for the strongest wood. Firi was honoured with the prize for her most stunning decorations. Juniper secured the warming spice award, while Pinely won the prize for her tasty nuts!

Nature's talent show lasted all day, and all the trees applauded for the other trees.

Interlude

Psalm 121 (A Psalm of David)[9]

1. I look up to the mountains. Where does my help come from?

2. My help comes from the Lord. He is the Maker of heaven and earth.

3. He won't let your foot slip. He who watches over you won't get tired.

4. In fact, he who watches over Israel won't get tired or go to sleep.

5. The Lord watches over you. The Lord is like a shade tree at your right hand.

6. The sun won't harm you during the day. The moon won't harm you during the night.

7. The Lord will keep you from every kind of harm. He will watch over your life.

8. The Lord will watch over your life no matter where you go, both now and forever.

[9] *Psalm 121:1-8 (https://www.bible.com/bible/110/PSA.121.NIRV) – New International Reader's version*

Later that evening, Hurricane Breaker blew in, bringing a storm that thundered and huffed and puffed through the whole forest. Some trees fell and were uprooted.

"Everyone, hold on tight! The storm will soon be over!" shouted Oaklan.

Larry was located close to the river, and the wet ground released him.

Feeling worried, Pinely cried out to the heavens and said, "Dear God, please help me! Save me from the scary storm. If you keep me safe, I'm going to thank you all my life. I know you can help me. Please!"

Later, the storm died down.

Larry Cedar rolled down the mountain.

Thump, bump ... "Someone help me!"

"Larry is in danger!" shouted Pinely,
stretching her branches out.

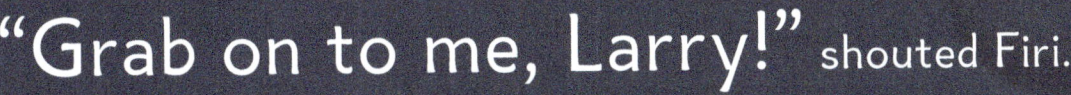

"Grab on to me, Larry!" shouted Firi.

Together, Pinely and Firi reached out to catch their friend, but none of the trees were strong enough to prevent Larry Cedar from falling.

In the morning, Deep Spring's water flowed to different areas of the forest, nourishing all the trees. However, it couldn't reach Larry.

Eventually, Larry's roots dried up, and he couldn't survive.

A few days later, foresters arrived to clear out the damaged trees.

They removed Larry Cedar and used his wood to build a bridge over Deep Spring. A sign on the bridge read: *"Long live Edenwild, the evergreen home for a blessed generation now and many to come."*

Larry Cedar would always be remembered through the bridge.

From then on, Deep Spring made its path through all the trees in the forest, ensuring they were all well watered.
Harmony returned to the trees of Edenwild, and they resumed their lives.

Some days later, the foresters came back.

"I heard a rattling sound earlier," said Oaklan.

"They planted a new shoot from the top stem of Larry Cedar!" exclaimed Firi.

"That was the branch that Pinely picked during the storm," mentioned Oaklan.

"Thank God!" said Pinely.

Everyone cheered.

"Are you still quitting, Pinely?" asked Juniper.

"With all that happened here, I don't think Pinely will want to stay," added Firi.

"Ah, not anymore! I'm blessed to be here," said Pinely. "Oaklan always says Edenwild is full of goodness and grace. Now I know it's true. This is our home!"

"We are blessed indeed!" cheered Oaklan.

"And we need each other!" said Pinely.
The trees clapped.

"Can we pray?" asked Juniper.

The trees bowed.

Juniper prayed, "Thank you, Lord. You made us and kept us safe from the storm. We had tough times, but you know best. Thanks for making us strong."

Pinely added, "Dear God, I'm forever grateful that you created me so perfectly. Thank you for restoring cedar and for watching us."

Pinely, Oaklan, Juniper, Firi, and Cedar were all beautiful and blessed. They looked radiant and lived happily ever after.

The trees sang their favourite chorus: "All things bright and beautiful, all creatures great and small; all things wise and wonderful, the Lord God made them all."[10]

[10]A public domain song written by Cecil F. Alexander

Fun Facts about the Trees[11]

Cedars grow as tall as 100 ft (30 metres) or more. They live very long, up to thousands of years.

Fir is one of the favourites used for Christmas trees! The fir bark and wood are used to make medicine.

Junipers belong to the Cypress plant family.
They grow as tall as 10 metres and can live up to 200 years.

Oaks are one of the most ancient trees that ever was on the earth. They are also one of the strongest woods in the world.

Pine trees are evergreens. They provide edible food like pine nuts, pine oil and pine bark flour, which is used to make pine bread in Sweden.

[11]The Woodland Trust.

Fun Facts about Spring Water[12]

Springs serve as natural sources of freshwater for humans. Spring water flows naturally from a place underground to the surface. For example, water from beneath rocks can emerge on the surface and create rivers.

There are several types of spring water, and they often contain minerals dissolved from rocks. These minerals are regarded as good for the body and health.

Rivers that originate from springs carry water from the land to the ocean. The ocean water then evaporates, forming clouds in the atmosphere. When the clouds become heavy, they release water as precipitation or rainfall onto the land. The water, in turn, flows back to the ground or finds its way back into rivers and smaller streams.

The continuous process of evaporation into clouds and precipitation to the earth is known as the water cycle.

[12] National Geographic Kids.

Activity Page

How to make toasted nut pancake:

1. Toast 20g of pine nuts in a pan, let it cool down and grind them in a blender.

2. In a large bowl, combine 50 grams of oat flour, 2 egg whites, 1 tablespoon of honey, and a splash of cinnamon.

3. Add half a teaspoon of baking powder and the ground pine nuts to the mixture in the bowl.

4. Pour 1 cup of your chosen type of milk.

5. For sweetness, add 10 grams of sugar and a pinch of salt.

6. Stir the mixture and set it aside.

7. Melt a small scoop of butter in a frying pan over low heat.

8. Pour some of the pancake mix into the frying pan.

9. Allow it to cook for about 3 minutes, flipping it to the other side for an additional 1 minute.

10. Transfer the pancake to a plate and enjoy it with your favourite topping!

Yum yum!

Colour and design your pancakes:

Can you write two things that God has blessed you with and that are amazing about you?

The Trees Friendship Chorus

"Friends forever, we're blessed forever,
Friends forever that's who we are!"

Can you compose your own friendship chorus or set a tune to the provided one and then share it with us? Use the hashtags #TreesFriendshipChorus and #BlessedAndBeautiful when sharing your creation.

More Books by Tayo Oshaye from Kids' Mini Psalm Book Series:
Vol. 1: *The Good Shepherd: Psalm 23*
Vol. 2: *I am Confident in God and Fearless: Psalm 27*

For more printables and free activities, visit our website at **www.joyfulpsalmskids.com**